The End of America

Book 8

Acknowledgements

Earlier versions of these poems appeared in *Across the Margin, Coconut, Manor House Quarterly, Poets for Change, Tacocat, Ecolinguistics, Capitalism Nature Socialism*, and the *100 Thousand Poets for Change Anthology*. Thanks to the editors.

The End of America Book 8
Copyright 2023 Mark Wallace

Design by Adam Deutsch

Glovebox Poems
San Diego, CA

First Edition
ISBN: 978-1-943899-16-6

All rights reserved. No part of this book may be reproduced without the publisher's written permission, except for brief quotations in reviews.

The End of America

Book 8

Mark Wallace

MERE innocence isn't enough

add some atrophy   rot, a dash

    fern root of old
        boy network

Notice helicopter wings beating
    ("could have been the fifth
        band member")

    Well, not "trapped,"
    not "water torture Guantanamo"

"Nice weather," I nod to the limping
guy twice a week for four years now

        Getting the button "mercenary
        for hire"
        after shooting
        my way through the checkpoint

    rub the paycheck
        filthy to see
        under the fine print

    Of course I'd rather
    woo you think
    I hate politics for fun?

    Want to
    give these gravestones
    a solid impression
        do the
    "naughty thing" on them
    during an endless tape loop Steely Dan
    30 Greatest Hits set

Never question the love language

                              it comes with
                and don't say "with" like
      any of us have
done that much
              this close

              to the high tech John Deere incinerator

      like for instance
              reading old Ann Landers advice

      columns into the void

      Pay me and let me
      get the after-midnight aura   train
                              one more bit

              I want to tear
              the world and heal
                              it at your feet

      before we move on to the info
      portion

DO you picture
it with yourself
                        in it?

        Or off to the
                      beach photo panel

     one more chance to be
                            untouched

tidal wave this way, wildfires that
        blip in the total economy (of need?),
    people served
           up

Look to the bright side and blink
      "Insert Optimism, Hit Button"

      Sunlight gothic when I got drunk
        the way *Birth of a Nation*
        made the KKK cool

                  going up close for a
                  picture of the funnel

I walked to the hilltop
    got the text
        that said the doctor won't let you
                drive
            makes options short
            in the back end suburbs

     working grocery store flowers
           or the Borders Book Desk

                      not much
                      left

      I guess there's a way
      of being
                in the flashback moment
                        only so much
                    chance to go around

         and the dry ground matchstick

I guess sometimes it uses us up

  before we do it
                to ourselves

TOWELS, tee-shirts, shorts
    blue black gray

  against the gray-painted balcony

      blue trash cans beyond
      on the pavement

not reflecting many little deaths

       in the isolated

      mind, some forgotten
      promising artist graduated

  to her meds, her doctors
  telling her not to leave the house

    The suburbs hides
      its drifters in late night
        "can't sleep" basements

  Child adult of adult child
      motorcycle 60s dream
      updated Tennessee waltz

    Poets in cities hiding out
      sheafs with ideas
    late night talk
      after the data entry office

  "Changed World" sign
  streaking away from the rear
  car window view

       somewhere between

    this room and that

STATE distribution
            under contest
                        by Blemish

        Free Inc.

                    long shadow
                    my legs walking
                            away from the ocean

            as if a poet could
                        ever want silence

White
hand painted
on stone, the need
        to trace effect,
                that "someone will know"

                        as if silence was not
                        what words have to reach

            What is it you
            don't want me to see?

                        This breezy suburban sunset
                                each person
                    in the home, not at home?

                One walking quiet
                towards the night ocean

                    "maybe give the money to charity"

Enough rage to take it nowhere
                        to fall off

                    to write straight into the hungry
                    world never on camera

landscape of small enclave discouragement
   termite-eaten

            When I talk to you I know
            what here is

BEAUTY tape loop trapped
beach condo baby

        court ruling
        star bellwether

      hip thrusting feverish loan
      straight through Orange County

    to set at least one brain free
    from the bog, just how they do it

with a received message,
cracked knees eighty-on-the-dollar

            hidebound referendums
           paining on the bandstand

      applause,
      usual range of dignitaries

            unleash
            clotted

            how to

DON'T want to
    "get it"
                please, universe

                      awe me

                      one

                      more time

Gathering emotional referendum blocked
    too many party lines

                a country floundering
                      on three or four back

            room deals

    Debt for wars, banks, cars
        not a cent for health care

THIRD Pope in Escondido
                        I've met this week
      local bushwhacking
      camera-ready cream

              New Logo Ship has sailed

Boring enough to work at The Center
      without hugging the machinery, trying to hear

            myself breathe
                  under a star-filled
        back country sky just west
                      of the old
                        artillery tower

Is it sex if you "own" it?
                  Deed to the deed

            "Get the government
                      out of my traffic jam"

            sort of like Beauty
                        and an extra sparkly
                  high tech Beast going

     at each other like a runaway bidding
          war in a rain-soaked Guatemalan airfield

I've listed ways
to profit off chrome
      piled in pre-planned obsolescence

                and I wanna make
                you love it so rough

              that I'm not stuck here holding
                  a final flimsy cautious dream

                    telling others how to live
              because they don't see
                            like I want

   Let's all do some heavy lifting
            another

              one note easy-to-say-it whisper
                            I tell

     people I don't know in bars

buy it, pack it
tote it around

    learn to spin it on plates

        END user license agreement
                        on loan

                Someone who doesn't understand
                        is listening right
                                now behind the palm
                                fearing a take-
                                over like it's not been
                                        taken already

        World leaders gather, authentic faces
                        lay bets on your brother's
                broken-info hoedown hassle
                        memory like it's got big

                        absence worth selling

        Gotta mention the mystical death panels
                a savings event at Ethan Allen

                                don't love myself so
                                need dozens
                                        to lie there and take it

Ghaddafi's tent pulled down in New Bedford
                you need to watch
                        what terrorist you bed beside
                                after you deal for his billions

        I've been in touch all day
                can't accept infinity
                        even between my toes

                not bent not broken just part
                        scheming like a static-
                        heavy wire

        swallowing a mouthful more
                                of death

12

        forever's cheap side

        No wonder I want
     The Loch Ness Monster

                and ten dollar
                      quarter rolls

"Never yank my laundry
out and put it on a dirty dryer top
ever again, you got that?
Signed, Anonymous"

SHOWSTOPPER—

    Insurance companies bloated with cash

nothing moving
    "accusing you of the thing I've done"
        "just want my seat in the corner
    close to the flood
        and fire statistics"

    We have ways of making you like it
        fast serve, cold serve
            antidepressant TV

    Time to turn up a transcendent
        view: military
            cargo ship bright in the harbor

        or men playing powerball
        with undergraduate voting rights

    so much relentless
    sagging recorded

        on the funding unit clipboard

        feel the draft
        through the closing door?

    America, I don't know
anything of those you leave
        picturing themselves to you
    in the waning bankroll night

        I'll wander down
        to the ocean and sit
        on the wall beside
            the concrete

causeway, dreaming
    of my own arm in some
        other arm, the last

  and best noble goal

        grinding my teeth

NO school for you, no job

        You're welcome

        No one in the house will stop
                        the house

                falling

Backed into a corner
white hot

"SEND the problem to someone else"

    twitching in the clenched jaw
        vocabulary indifference

            costs of avoided potential

                library closed
                hallway lights off

    Governor Body Builder handing Exxon
      cash with a "Who Me?" grin

                decay by design
                "The Promise"

TRAPPED escapist end of day
splintered beside a bed
                         worthless dollars

            What would God tell
                  me to sell off

       For instance, on the line
       between legal
                   and illegal back seat
                   descriptive terminology loss
                   your hand felt hot—

Zero hour, nowhere
thoughts to
             send the need pushing back

Skateboarders sitting inside the parked
                   big gas SUV
                      mouth words at the windows
    (my attempts to find someone to talk with)—

                      won't know, I imagine—

          Goodbye Mr. Federman
          I hung around
                    the Internet looking
                    at writer death notices,

             watching baseball

        Bureaucracy always describes
                 itself
             no groveling floor-ridden sun-seeking eyes

                             needing method,
                             streets to walk down

             earth an awkward

   species   I wanted to touch

      vision to make
          some
          connection to you

loved and lost and loved and didn't
    want to do it again
        in any lost middle
    dark to see it flash

   another note about money

         instead

         of blood or air

LYING face first
in the sand sick
        of lacking power

    corporate rollerball craphouse

        religion and weapons, media info barrage,
            people encouraged
        to vote against
their own material needs

        a stranger
        in the country where
            I've lived my life

The flat hot walls
of housing complexes, chain stores,
    beach front mansions always empty,

    homes foreclosed
in sunny mystical vibrant air

        Wanting and able to survive
        even as others go under, I

        stomach quivering…

A society that hates societies
    will always at last undo itself

        I'm a poet of the moon
        I want to show you its other side,

        to talk to you in a world
    transformed by our feeling through it

Instead I say one
    in eight with no money, one
    in eight with no job

        too late to be late
            for some western dream sky

          Old VW bus
    wobbling down the road
        towards Car
            Dealership Canyon

On the other side, I'll be standing
long after this world
        leaves me for dead

     crushing the rubble, scraping the dead
        skin with bare hands

using tinfoil, hair, plastic and charcoal
    to make art into

          forgotten monuments

              instead of more scheduled

                  cast-out days

"WHY does our neighbor think we
      drive too fast, why does he call
the cops instead
          of speaking to us personally?"

                    "Fourteen Somalian Villages
                        Agree to Stop Female
                            Genital Mutilation"

      almost sometimes seem to be telling

                infinity, street sign

          Monday inability to

                    "pen and notebook are personal
                    items no writing at Vons"

          lens named "emotional distance"

      won't tell it in Philly, won't
            drop it on Berkeley

                              "consumers for once
                              could benefit"

TAKE me inside the conference
room at Insurance Company X

     after romanticism dies
     monopoly by new
       constructed feelings

  as if last night's Heaven
    at the Happy Hour

doesn't translate in discourse

    theory when compared to a guy

  choosing the proper spreadsheet carefully

      cashed out

 in a thought

    "that's just too much"

     Not knowing the Marines
      in the beachfront bar,
        trying to think

    while they shout and sing

    along with Journey's "Don't

     Stop Believin'"

 my brain still stuck
 in a long week's final

    creeping production molasses maneuver
       just as I take

    off for the weekend

    will inspiration be gluten-free?

                        Untenable world

          I'm empty
          nothing even tragic about it

          like discovering it's somebody
                    else's turn

       to go right through the Honda
                    skylight to commune

                with a multi-legged God

back to Cleveland?

                Robin Hood in Reverse

    perverse incentives

                  This time you
            be labor, I'll be
            management

surrounded by curly-haired
        snack girls with prescribed futures
    to give me energy to utter conditions

down your computer's spine

        the universe a small batch
    backorder
                doing it again

        banning photos
              civilian death

>   It's good to know you're
>   not playing politics
>
>   splashing unsuspecting children
>   at bus stops like they asked
>   for it in the rainstorm
>
> Later you'll find me at the bar
>   drinking down significance
>
>   that arrived in the mail
>   just yesterday
>
>   Today we have a new action figure
>   thick enough to stuff with fire
>
>   it wears us out only when ashes
>
>   remind us what we've burned

WIRES crossed across the public
       selling

    Temps Available
           costlier parking

  "Don't even pretend I'm
       the one responsible"

    Found myself in the wrong
          interrogation room

   people waiting for an eight-
  headed ecstasy dog
      "gotta make 'em want it, right?"

Like the nerves I felt
   had been choreographed by distant
    rats pushing
      buttons for food

   after I paid for contemplation
       in official degree form

If my back
   yard is all that interests
      me in the post-
        garage sale fever

  going high speed all over
     this beach town's bountiful
       system for directing traffic

    towards the non-free

  zone, the ever more slender boutique
       that each of us

                        imagine ourselves up
                                    against

It doesn't take batteries
        It gets adjusted
                from the digital booth

No wonder people long
                to be naked

            in boisterous prominence

property values in their
                flip-switch control

        all the microphones
                calibrated

to the tiniest rhythmic variation
            in anyone's hidden universe

OVERBLOWN metal detector
    flycatcher rat man

        clear plastic shirt flapping

      in sandy beach breeze, focuses his
          housing-demon-infused dementia—

I'm washed up
        in some gargantuan
           factory-fresh dream

    visioning equality
which benefits my
    side just a bit,

      see-sawing through the practical
        terms for
        adding and splitting

No one wants to be
    the lonely old one leaning
      on rocks carefully

          arranged above the beach
              adjust to the right

              angle to feel
              poignant

People trying to escape
        themselves

    being that one, no other

    the possible always skirted
      with impossible boundaries

in which so much

can happen and so
                much can't

      Vast electrical charge
            bone, muscles and skin

that thrives by wearing
              itself out

                      the familiar spark
                      its own flaring
                            up and vanishing

What can it do
      even to mention it

Wanting to walk there
            with you
            to know it too?

HOME is where
         I hide out, guns drawn
     waiting for Adobe Flash Player

           or a phone call to slip
                     abstract money out
                           of my abstract

             image of myself. Tried to define

    a tree and realized
            I don't know much about

        whose terms I've been
        borrowing
                  to steal some fire-

  breathing into a complacent
            system just for getting

everything over with.
What would Captain Kirk do?

                   In this space
            ship I should be saving—

      people inside
          who try to explore—

      Still I'm asking what
               it costs to imagine

        any universe burgeoning

        beyond the limits it knows

I don't mind you living
           in your body
     except the ceiling's pushing lower

inside this little mini-
              van filled with overpriced
        non-working gadgets.

Fresh peaches
    in the morning won't

        and not much else

This offer, its managerial savvy

            from a couple guys in cowboy gear

may fund armies in the golden
    triangle international
             funds exchange

I've still lost
        the beautiful moment
            touching my forehead

        to the stars

        that weren't much more
        than operatives with a budget

who taught me how
        to set up accounts

    and watch the money

             come in in smaller

chunks than would even

        be worth defending

SEEKING a little
    restrained horror
   with a noirish Southern California

        real estate scam
        context

suitable for reframing a private
     crumbling vision

        Community Resource Center
          in a drop down

    last chance menu

    before the highway goes double
      wide right through the breastbone

in-bred sonic isolation
     that roars good when it catches

   your dreams with their pants
     down around your neighbor's ankles

How badly do you want
     to live

    to feel your skin pressed against

      the vanishing surfaces
       big fog

    pushing in over the empty
      newly-rebuilt beach front

mansions and three-room condos
    could be metaphor

   the aging body

        without ever saying

how each is caught
        up in the other

      "alone" another form of connection
           that regulation attempts

      to label in an ownership
           maneuver,

        "my breath," "your eyes,"

    tidy quiet suburban afternoon
        inside a swath cut

      by carefully organized
             death;

Take a little cancer sample
        your tongue's underside

      officially permitted

    replacement for a learning moment
        about anything going on

down at the speedway, bets are placed
    Exxon in five, no mojo for Kabul

Up on the hill, grasses blow
    until they're kindling-dry

    and some thirsty boy

      dizzy

    lights them like he thinks he's the universe

NEW countries get old
                    fast as legal rights

     can be stripped
            out of any gung-ho document barreling

through people-funded government that funds
           those same corporations you're

                stuck in the 5 p.m.
        traffic watching, cars crawl past the glass

    Windowed, late-construction functional

         office park   inflated product thinking

   In moist darkening air
            the fog looks exactly
                      like smoke
       from burning buildings

       Stop a moment and pick
            your teeth, clean the sweat

      off the files you find yourself
           holding regarding
                a tire-slashing former Marine

   who's allowed to go on
           serving parents and teaching students

These lotteries a little short
           on people   Bundled cash

              may itself be the ticket

                    for pursuing yourself
                        branded, resting

    on laurels and easy deals
                  that inflame a West-East

        split whose discomfort
              is comforting, graspable

    like the notion that we're
        each the center of our own

              epic, the epicenter
                  of an earth that comes

    landsliding down the mountain
              wanting it that way

        Hold on, there's only one
            of each of the others

    on this two-month tape
        playing repeatedly

        in the so-inclined heads

        gearing up to run
                a world straight

    against its own best dreams

FROM total confidence to total
         collapse quicker than a freeway
                      can stop when an airplane

    crashes onto it;

    guess these
             people alone in cars
                          won't be going

      anywhere except their spot
                just right there   the radio

    wraps up what nobody's
                  getting any time soon
 now that members of Congress receive

                      their speeches directly
                                  from Genentech,

      subsidiary of the Swiss drug giant
                      Roche, not to be

 confused with the Belgians
                  who bought Budweiser

              Even Comic-Con is sold
                     out of the bargain four-
                            day passes may I mention

        the blow-up elephant in the blow-
                      up media room

 the choices themselves
           do the choosing, basically cheating

         then taking the chance to blame the Chinese

                     for actually making

                    tires, toothpaste, plastic, pipe

    Maybe a run will burn
                these words out, later

            from the battered head
                    reception unit going

by my name, assumed and genuflecting

                            at properly
                            calibrated intervals

        A person, say, is one
                    of the options passed up

    at the latest corporate government shindig

                How am I going
                    to know you

                        more than as patron
                                    to "service"

Back when I believed
        there was no future to hope for and now
                there is and I don't

                    know which is more confusing

One more time at the Costume
        Reinduction Ball, you as cat, me
                            as clown

        plotting to tie up the whole
                ball of wax and burn it

                            another
                            long ago story

  I tell to no one while stuck
     looking at the wings of a twin
      engine Cessna

    a man at least
    with a notebook and no

      time that he's going to be anywhere

ANOTHER 21st century
        citizen trying not
                to die in place

    dreaming of some
        other hand to touch
                in replacement for familiar

productive time

grabbing behind the tract
    a chance to live
        that doesn't already

        feel like description
            of every move

as a function of a fine-
        tuned instrument made

    of these streets
            "I could get on the freeway, go
                straight out into

        my current life mirrored

                as long as I don't
                    have to keep

                living this one"

    Legs shoving shoes
    tightly into the gravel
    I walk down
        the hillside
            the path below

        the ridge lined

       with houses

              some with carport,
              pool, high fence,

    myself, breathing
    comparing me

            to dead again again

        I don't stop, today

                  in a picture
                  I don't yet become

SOME countries disappear
        poets, grab

     them from their beds
        or some floor

   in a cramped
        neighborhood where people light
                fires and burn leaders

in effigy, where men
        in black cars with no

     plates suddenly stop

beside an apartment
     where a young poet leaves
                a room

     and poems, forever

             There, because of it

             the poems matter, or seem to

Here, poets

        go to coffee houses, art galleries, bars
                read their poems

        angry or sad or gut-shot funny

                no one

        takes them anywhere
                secretly or against
                        their will

they publish books and men

in blog

comments say none
of it matters

the poems kill
no one the poems
save no one

certainly not the poets themselves

as if the bloggers
believe they understand

that only death

can make a poem
live

that those who don't
wrongly die need
to know

that any escape just equals irrelevance

—it's inside this wrongness,
love,

that I try
to live

in the poem and in

whatever air

is left

TAKING pictures by the one hundred
          foot brontosaurus at Cabazon

    windmills
          churning in the dusty
                pass on the valley's

edge the human-created
          motion highlighting

      the concrete

    unfreedom everyday

    "nothing's stopping you
              from living homeless"

    "if you wish"

Reminding others
        of the options   the limits

        He tries to turn
                education into a wild

          cat day trader speculation

                    bubble

    vibrating to the whim
          of corporate-raiding barracudas

    Guys in Martinsville Ohio
              working night

        shifts installing freezer

    lights for a grocery store
              national chain using

                              part-time

                workers with no
                          benefits or security

            exploding numbers

                and a food stamp

                          beneficiary growth curve

                                    hidden suburban
                                              poor
    "I always thought
            people on public

                          assistance were lazy, put

                                    piles of steaks
                                    in their shopping carts,

                    but it helps

                    feed my kids"

        Clinging
              to an ideology until
                                    it abandons
                              the way it was meant to,

        you become abandoned,
                          rejecting yourself

                    Still, a weekend
                              out of town clears

                                        the brain

prepared to be right
back at it

BACK town gray

    just in it for the thrill
        soundtrack, half
            meant attempt at seeming

    one of any
    group thinking itself

        one, not far

also from any thirteen
    newly formed wrinkles

or degrading who much
        wants to know

the woman eating dog food over the holidays
    a block away
from the Business Transit

        Center, o vast commuter
system its abandoned dream

    some possible working
    together. Quick eat at the Pita

        Pit and off

to the park where nobody
    knows me again

    isolated self/unscripted other
        human-need panorama

    a few rough-bearded, half-sane men
        hovering nearby
            over a grill with chicken

   smoke floating up
        into the oaks and overcast
                resort afternoon.

     No one's disinvesting

             in things that only seem
               "as they are"

   Yard-by-yard chain
      to make a segment disappear

into its own complacent photo,

    people   "having fun"   "in the camera"

right after the train pulls out, whistling.

If love is the only needed word
I'll never know it

         on this day, gnats
             drinking in heavy

     air

       Want what you want,
            there was never another

way to be any small part
      this uncontainable restless

     drive to connect to the physical
        instant, turning earth

    that may finally get gassed
       by its own

      or go on giving birth

                to which officials
                assign meaning

        without

   permitting anything
         else it might be

CHRISTMAS yesterday

    nothing in
    my brain wants

    to stay
    in itself

At the beach
    families walk under
        clouds and through

    momentary gusts

    dogs slip into
    low surf's edges

I can't take
      the bombs out
    of the poem or really
            put them in

      With death and life
      one is always at each

        moment the more
           abstract

    like I can
      only love you with you or

        without you

      never both
        always

      both always

      what's here and isn't

                    as if anyone
            could shut it out or keep
                            it in,

    ocean moving

        far from my bench

        above this anonymous bluff

HAPPY
completion of another

        cycle in the Western
                Calendar System

    the gesture
        adds to some

portion of this
        body
                finding "itself"

        cracked, cheerful, expostulating

        some truth that's "itself"

to sustain
        the feet moving they'll move

                anyway, it's not

            avoidable

by putting on headphones and staring
    along the shore
             stroking one's beard

      in a moment's
           "got you" wisdom about decay

    not much use
    trying to be right

             people's minds stuffed with
            ideas

on paper made in factories

families and couples strolling
					past to available

		restaurants and bars

			January 1, 2010

		hoisted on a banner

CELL phone gives
                    me unwanted advice

               about the day:

"prone to miscommunication"   "overly sensitive"

          I don't walk
                  by the train tracks don't

               go into stores

     Escape from grandly
             celebrated interlocking
                  traffic that brings

"us all" into closer proximity

             is it possible
             to burn like what's not?

Politics and the practice
      of fear
                  manipulation and football

    Insert a blank

CD, acknowledge unexpected distance

            sun against the slats

imagine a restructured economy
not founded on ownership

                   play some Ella Sings Duke

There is no place not
          on the continuum

                being present

        through a body-mind not simply
                                    belonging

    couches and wine   available splurging
                                      on screen

              comfort parade
                        convenient payment options

PROFIT down,
        the value of profit
        up, moments passing

    into the hollow
             in other moments

        Inside an office
           sun long and low
                    over high surf

      It's not the mind
         transforms
              the mind, brings the body

    out of grooves and what not to notice

          Protected transcendent beach
              spot doesn't freeze

    itself doesn't keep
        the inside out

        and if I want   the outside
                              in?

  It's funny that walking
        should be a belief

            passing through in contact

      with others

      It's not
      politics to know
            that the body drifts away

    impossible irresponsible

                        staying

urgent pull
          feet forward

                    to embrace
                    what's coming towards

me even when I don't

          try to meet it

cars shimmering past
                    the Encina Power Plant

          concrete rising behind
                    a fence and looming above

                    high wave rolling

                    down the coast

DOWNTOWN San Diego

just enough
    city for some to think

        it is one

      With one last day
        to be away

          from my public self

      I see Tina Donovan's
      wall-sized plastic straw
           texture art

walk the trolley-side sidewalks, climb
      Banker's Hill eat lobster tacos
    ("in San Diego everything's

a taco, in D.C. a burger")

      traveling
        to take the brain out

    from what it ordinarily
    overlooks

Tomorrow I will look

        expected in the expected
           rotation corner

    the soul's full hockey gear
      strapped to my scaffold

      There's no
        time more than what
        we do with it

					no way to run away
					from these figments
												body

among Irish and tequila pubs

							striving to resist

							its own clutches

FILE conversion banter
                    translates the dark

                    brain half into formats

    useful for a new

reshaped decade
        tools for the instituted moment

                    with rechargeable love
                    devastation packages

          voice logo added
              over all non-authorized

    illusory visions
    laying out deciduous night

                even when randomly

installed by the fevered adjacent
      trademarked real human flesh

that never could control
              its longing to break the data ID

    bracelet attached to every breath's flutter

motion censure time-cost mechanism
      feeding back bits

                of the person
              one might once have been

            through distortion principle layers
                  hiding fees

    until level three breakdown interiors

        sing "electric electric"

        100 Swedish

        techno backup singers

welcoming you to abandon

                      yourself to the category
                      "heart's music"

            chiming in another era's

            one-stop two-stop phony
                            authenticity

                        with horns

BOUGHT-SPEECH outback
                      among mudslide hills
         there are no jobs to move
                        anyone's economy
              Security for the walled-off
                            neighborhood riding
in a truck in half-hour circles
                    some closed down imported
      detox backstreet blight
                        spread out
in random nicked bits
                      50-year old man
     breaks into his daughter's
                    college roommate's
           bedroom
           accuses her of taking
his whole country from underneath
                      his earthquake-ridden
                                stock-market ground
     like an explosion of restraining
                  orders on the universe
Go ahead and hang
           yourself every day
     and call it some other
                  dead person's fault

If air was sucked up
    as much as money

        —the earth a mangled purple—

    whose tongue would speak
                its own name
        like it was yours

        Voice of a CEO
            triangulated for all

      three government divisions

    echoing themselves above
        collapsing tin coffers

      data slopped

    into a drone deal

whose terms won't be heard or even discussed

            Meanwhile, lovers

    bow down before those
        they don't even
        know yet—

      arid waste where flesh
            still wants water

VALENTINE'S

Never has so little
    a holiday tormented
        so many

    People out in a frenzy
        warm weather and romantic

    intentions fit to norms—

that tired-on-a-Sunday
        unfocused-concrete-unfreedom

    down-in-the-sunlight blues

  one step from starting

  one's role again in the systematic
        removal from the physical

    until the face
        stretches itself to aching;

Languid in the moment, almost liquid
        as if dissolving

    therefore not yet gathered again

        wanting as a way
        to get out

  and finely attuned
        to anything wrong

a persona of one's own feelings
    surging through the stopgap
        last insisting sense, nothing

coming to the rescue

        why no one can know themselves
        too much of the time

ferris wheel dream

picture that turning

as a way to get walking
        back into the ineluctable

    static

SONG segments, slammed
          against a per-dollar slicing

      into a supplicant-mendicant

   game who's hiding

      behind each expert
          marketing statement stalemate

      No wonder love

becomes its own rhetorical slathering

   and you and I go

      place to place, shopping,
      selling

         debating the open air
            hanging just above

   the steering-locked Toyota

      the specifics exactly
         one more Meg Whitman ad

and taking 8 pills a day for 10 days

      I don't have

      any language to get us out
         or back in

         no way to turn the ceaseless

            dividing

         I watch you

move past me and me past you
and me past me and you past you

    dizzy and speeding

        There's no safety, no protection
                in the glass, brick, tin

      counting

   pieces lined up
      in easy choosing rows

LEARNING
           how to wake up today

                      and decide why
                                  later

      no dream and no example

              pure divorce

              One moment
                        we were there together

                                and then

UNDERCOVER
>   shopping at the local Rite Aid

>   think spread, lather, swallow

as price-chopped workers
>   wander away

>   from counters, kneel low

>   in aisles, tapping watches

>   to see when time
>   runs out they're

>   "people with jobs" "according
>   to latest figures"

At college the entering freshmen
>   often have trouble

>   supporting their children, finding
>   a second job nights...

Running through fields, dreaming
>   of being touched,

>   the shopper's
>   half-torn mind hears moon-sung concerts

>   sees bountiful flesh, brandless fantasias

>   anything to lose the body
>   back into
>   memory of itself

>   anything not to see

>   his own hand on the glass door's handle

taking him out
            into the day's

        next parcel

BOMB found in narcissistic
    freefall

  Industrial captains throwing
     panic buttons
        to the panicked
      night-dream time bomb

    cannibal frenzy

   The number to dial
      when there's no

     reason for calling,

   voting for one to keep
      another away

    in the human discard business,

  in some gone survivalist
     TV screening photo shoot

   you might call
     undefined environment waste

     dislocating stray knees

  and removing history
     from books in Texas

Attention, drivers countrywide,

    Please Turn Off

   anything that tries to tell
     you anything by the retaining

    money buckets

just as the brights

        get blinding

CORPORATE heads trying
   to buy political

  office on 480
      cable channels

 computer figures clacking down

 on the heads of whoever tries

   to decipher
     the language or doesn't

 a great looping
    philosophy that says
one thing or its exact
    opposite
    whenever relevant;

   future a clashing
   of concepts that play

  with your cunts, cocks, assholes

 with the nerve
   stimulation centers
      in your bombarded brains

   and mine

constant info-data cycle fed

  intravenously

 what you do
 about it always slower—

    ah, it's our sex we use up

                         exhausting ourselves

        in not being able to often know

                      what and why we do

           sheer physical surge
                   of one and other

      that airways teach
            about how to exchange

America's virgins are depressed

                 never dressing themselves for

         any high-command technological rubbing

                   A man shouts
                   "Monster," never knowing

          a man has hit him

               bodies on waves

   —as if seeing my hand
                  in a mirror,

                 my face no clue

         to what I'm thinking

    when I don't want "fight"
               to be the metaphor

          and don't know how
                to describe

a meal among

starvation

INTERGALACTIC waste particles

    filter through rain

    into a timely stew

        that brings the universe

close in every instant, multiple

        dimensions and planes
            angling through bodies

  in rotation on a money

        wheel that distributes
            uneven access

across the up-to-the-minute landscape

        refracted onto screens

  at ye olde counting house refurbished

        for some baseline banks-
            as-bookies fraud,

  build the neighborhood

        to topple and make side

            bets on the toppling, both ends

collapsing the middle strategic

    underpinning
    in the back closet corner

        of each public oil

        spillage info leak

   That's all I have, sister, brother

            "free world" rhetoric marked

        ink under skin

That each of you matters—

      the line I'd always

      hoped to end on

                September 2009-May 2010

ALSO BY MARK WALLACE

The End of America, Book Fifteen (Glovebox Books, 2021)
The End of America, Book Three (Glovebox Books, 2018)
Crab (Submodern Books, 2017)
Notes from the Center on Public Policy (Altered Scale Press, 2014)
The End of America, Book One (Dusie Kollectiv, 2012)
The Quarry and The Lot (BlazeVox, 2011)
Felonies of Illusion (Edge Books, 2008)
Walking Dreams: Selected Early Tales (BlazeVox, 2007)
Temporary Worker Rides A Subway (Green Integer, 2004)
Haze: Essays, Poems, Prose (Edge Books, 2004)
Dead Carnival (Avec Books, 2004)
Oh Boy (Slack Buddha Press, 2004)
The Monstrous Failure of Contemplation with Aquifer by Kaia Sand (self-publish or perish, 2001)
My Christmas Poem (Poetry New York, 1998)
Nothing Happened and Besides I Wasn't There (Edge Books, 1997)
Sonnets of a Penny-A-Liner (Buck Downs Books, 1996)
In Case of Damage To Life, Limb, or This Elevator (Standing Stones, 1996)
The Haunted Baronet (Primitive Publications, 1996)
The Lawless Man (Upper Limit Music, 1996)
Every Day Is Most Of My Time (Texture Press, 1994)
Complications From Standing In A Circle (Leave Books, 1993)
You Bring Your Whole Life To The Material (Leave Books, 1992)
By These Tokens (Triangle Press, 1990)

www.ingramcontent.com/pod-product-compliance
Lightning Source LLC
Chambersburg PA
CBHW030348100526
44592CB00010B/877